D1519067

CUTTING-EDGE TECHNOLOGY

3-D PRINTERS

James Bow

Gareth Stevens
PUBLISHING

Please visit our website, **www.garethstevens.com**.
For a free color catalog of all our high-quality books,
call toll free 1-800-542-2595 or fax 1-877-542-2596.

Cataloging-in-Publication Data

Names: Bow, James.
Title: 3-D printers / James Bow.
Description: New York : Gareth Stevens Publishing, 2017. | Series: Cutting-edge technology | Includes index.
Identifiers: ISBN 9781482451672 (pbk.) | ISBN 9781482451610 (library bound) | ISBN 9781482451498 (6 pack)
Subjects: LCSH: Three-dimensional printing–Juvenile literature.
Classification: LCC TS171.8 B69 2017 | DDC 621.9'88–dc23

First Edition

Published in 2017 by
Gareth Stevens Publishing
111 East 14th Street, Suite 349
New York, NY 10003

© 2017 Gareth Stevens Publishing

Produced for Gareth Stevens by Calcium
Editors: Sarah Eason and Harriet McGregor
Designer: Jessica Moon
Picture researcher: Rachel Blount

Picture credits: Cover: Getty Images: Günay Mutlu (photo), Shutterstock: Eky Studio (banner), Shutterstock: R-studio (back cover bkgrd); Inside: Flickr: Creative Tools (CC BY 2.0) 1, 39, Bre Pettis (CC BY 2.0) 5, U.S. Army RDECOM (CC BY 2.0) 41; Shutterstock: ArtThailand 13, Lucadp 36, Dario Sabljak 29, Sspopov 11, Stefano Tinti 17, 23, WeStudio 21; Wikimedia Commons: Jost Amman 9, Globaloria Game Design (CC BY-SA 2.0) 45, HIA (CC BY-SA 3.0) 30, Fred Hsu (CC BY-SA 3.0) 33, Jynto (CC0 1.0) 42, Philip James de Loutherbourg/The Yorck Project 7, Makerbot Industries (CC BY 2.0) 27, Saskia2586 (CC BY-SA 3.0) 35, Stephen Shephard (CC-BY-SA-2.5) 19, Studio Under (CC BY-SA 3.0) 25, S Zillayali (CC BY-SA 3.0) 14.

Printed in the United States of America
CPSIA compliance information: Batch #CS16GS: For further information contact Gareth Stevens, New York, New York at 1-800-542-2595.

CONTENTS

CHAPTER 1

PRINTING

This book looks at three-dimensional (3-D) printers, a technology that could revolutionize the way things are made. 3-D printers allow designs to be downloaded from the Internet and printed in your own home. Anything can be printed, from plates and cups to artificial limbs.

CHANGING LIVES

3-D printers are changing lives throughout the world. People in developing countries often have little money and may be far from roads that can transport goods. By introducing 3-D printers to these countries, the people there can make what they need rather than having to buy it and have it transported to them.

Po Paraguay, in Paraguay, is an organization that is changing people's lives by using 3-D printing. It is a nonprofit organization set up to provide **prosthetic** limbs at low cost. It uses a 3-D printer to create the limbs, making them more quickly and for less money than would be possible with other machines.

CUTTING EDGE

In 2014, a young girl named Lalyz moved the fingers on her right hand for the first time. Born without a hand, her parents took her to Po Paraguay. Lalyz's arm was scanned with a laser that took measurements of the arm. Then a 3-D printer laid down thin layers of plastic to the measurements taken and produced parts of a hand. Once cooled, these parts were put together to make a hand with moving fingers.

Plans for this MakerBot 3-D printer can be downloaded, allowing the user to build their own 3-D printer.

The journey to the creation of 3-D printers has been a long one. In the early days of civilization, when people wanted to make things, they used materials from the world around them. They wove small branches into walls. They broke larger branches to make fires. They figured out that mud could be mixed with water and left to dry to form bricks. They found that if they heated the mud in hot ovens, it became even harder and could be used to make pottery.

TOOLS

Making objects was slow work. Objects were produced one at a time, and many people were needed to make objects in large quantities. Over time, people learned how to improve their methods as they worked. They discovered that by using tools made from sticks and stones they could work more quickly and more easily.

MACHINES

Eventually, the tools people used became machines that required power to provide the energy to do work. The earliest machines used water for power to turn wheels. Then people figured out how to boil water and use the steam for power to push presses that could shape metal. This was the start of the Industrial Revolution, which began in the 1700s.

By the early nineteenth century, the Industrial Revolution had changed the world through the invention of machines. Because machines could quickly do work that would once have taken dozens of people a long time to do, more people had time to work on other things. People invented new technologies and made more goods. People's lives became better and more comfortable.

The 1801 painting *Coalbrookdale by Night* by Philip James de Loutherburg shows the furnaces and big buildings needed to make things at the start of the Industrial Revolution.

INDUSTRIAL REVOLUTION

The Industrial Revolution brought about changes that benefitted people, but it also brought changes that were not so good. The machines needed to make goods were big and could only operate in large factories. People had to buy goods produced by the factories, rather than make them themselves. This took away the power of people to produce what they needed individually. New, small 3-D printers now promise to give back this power.

A two-dimensional (2-D) printer is a printing press. Ink is rolled on blocks of metal that have been molded into letters. Paper is put over the inked letters and pressed against it, moving the ink onto the paper. The technology was invented in China and brought to Europe by the German Johannes Gutenberg (c.1390s–c.1468) in 1439. The technology allowed him to print books quickly and at low cost. One of the first books Gutenberg printed was the Bible.

Gutenberg's printing press changed the world. Before the press, books were made by hand. Monks would spend days copying text and drawing pictures, and they could only work on one book at a time. This meant that a handful of people had a lot of control over what was written and what was read. Gutenberg's press could print dozens of books in one day. Suddenly, there were more books to read, and more people started reading.

IDEAS SPREAD

With the invention of the press, ideas could be printed and passed around to a lot of people. Members of the Catholic Church wanted to control what people read. They tried to ban some books to keep people from reading them. However, the printing press had changed the world and it could not be changed back. People began to print newspapers and send letters. The printing press put many new scientific and political ideas into people's hands.

Just as 2-D printers made it possible for more people to share ideas, 3-D printers will make it possible for people to make things at home, without relying on big factories for goods. This will give people more independence and could change the world just as much as the printing press once did.

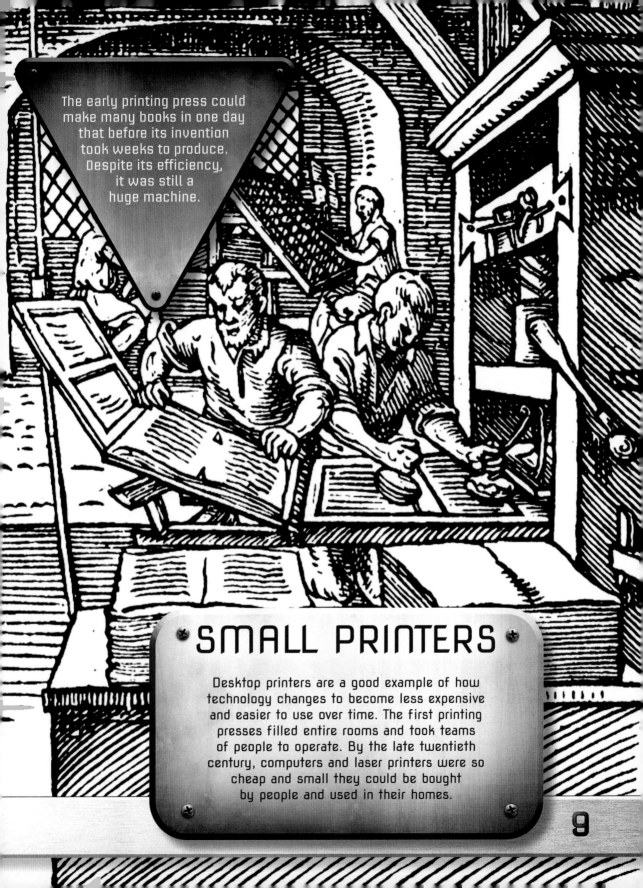

The early printing press could make many books in one day that before its invention took weeks to produce. Despite its efficiency, it was still a huge machine.

SMALL PRINTERS

Desktop printers are a good example of how technology changes to become less expensive and easier to use over time. The first printing presses filled entire rooms and took teams of people to operate. By the late twentieth century, computers and laser printers were so cheap and small they could be bought by people and used in their homes.

3 DIMENSIONS

A 2-D object is flat, like a piece of paper. You can print things on it, and it has length and width. A 3-D object has length and width, but it also has height. Adding height can be a challenge. A drawing on a piece of paper can only lie flat on a flat surface such as a table. To add a third dimension, you must build a structure that can resist the force of gravity. The earliest machines added height to structures made of metal by first melting the metal and then pressing it into molds. The molds shaped the hot metal into the shapes that people wanted, such as machine parts. The molds also supported the hot metal until it cooled and became solid enough to support itself.

REQUIREMENTS

Today, 3-D printers use materials that support their own weight. All 3-D printers have the same basic features. They need raw material to print with, they need to be able to turn the material into a shape people want, and they need a space in which to print.

CUTTING EDGE

One way that some 3-D printers work is by **sintering**. This is a process in which fine granules, or grains, are heated and pressed together, so they fuse, or join. The fine grains may be metal, plaster, or plastic, and lasers are used to accurately fuse the granules.

Making things takes a lot of energy and work. This milling machine becomes heated as it cuts metal and must be sprayed with water to keep it cool.

EARLY 3-D PRINTERS

3-D printers are a recent technology. Hideo Kodama invented the first 3-D printer in 1981 in Japan. This machine melted a plastic and then turned it into a desired shape. An **ultraviolet** light was shone on the structure to harden it.

Other early 3-D printers used lasers to carve objects out of solid material such as metal, plastic, or blocks of wood. These early machines were large and expensive. They were not machines that could be put inside a person's home. However, as lasers became more accurate, and as printer parts became smaller and easier to make, 3-D printing machines became smaller and cheaper. This then made it possible for more people to buy them for use in their homes.

3-D printers turn a raw material into an object. The raw material will determine how easy and expensive the object is to make and how durable it is. The raw material must be soft enough to be carved or melted, and it needs to be strong enough to support its own weight. There are many different materials that 3-D printers use, but they all fall into four categories: wood fiber, clay, **polymers**, and metal.

TYPES OF MATERIALS

Wood is flexible and strong. It can support a lot of weight and can be shaped by bending or carving. Wood is used to build houses and can be carved into bowls, plates, and artwork. Wood can be chopped into fibers and made into paper or wood composite. Composite acts just like wood, but its grain can be precisely controlled so that when it breaks under a 3-D-printing tool, it does so exactly in the way the printer operator desires.

Clay holds its shape when wet and becomes hard when dried or baked. This makes clay an excellent material for creating bricks, plates, and cups.

The polymer plaster is a fine powder of special sand that can be shaped when wet and forms a hard surface when dry.

CUTTING EDGE

Paper may not seem like a good building material. It is flexible, but it is thin—surely it cannot support its own weight? However, when layers of paper are pressed together, paper becomes strong. **Lamination** is a process in which layers of paper are built up and pressed together with glue. Some 3-D printers use paper and glue to build objects that are strong and durable. Laminated paper armor can withstand arrows!

Wood is an excellent material for carving things because it holds its shape while being carved, allowing artists to create a lot of small details.

Metal and plastic are used in 3-D printing. Metal is a solid that is hard and shiny and can bend without breaking. Metals are made of **atoms** or simple **molecules** that include metal atoms. In nature, they are usually found in a type of stone called an ore and mixed with nonmetal atoms such as oxygen or carbon. To get the metal out of the ore, people may put the ore through a process called **smelting**. The ore is heated in a furnace and the metals in the ore melt and separate. The parts that are not metal, called impurities, are left behind.

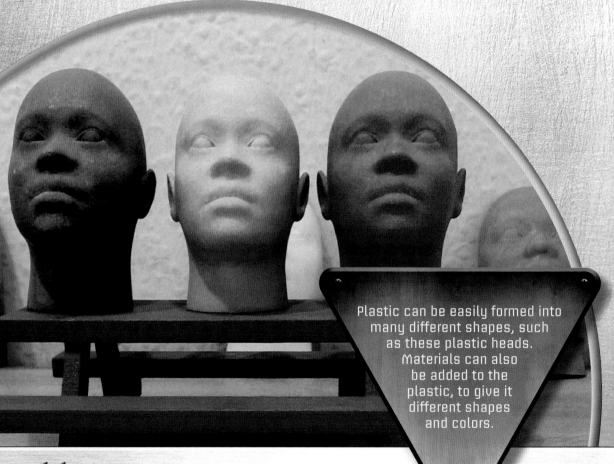

Plastic can be easily formed into many different shapes, such as these plastic heads. Materials can also be added to the plastic, to give it different shapes and colors.

RECYCLING

One big advantage of metal is that it can be recycled, or turned into something new. Because metals are atoms or simple molecules, a metal object can be melted into the raw material it was originally. Today, some plastics can also be recycled. This means that unwanted plastic objects can be recycled into new objects, which reduces damage to the environment.

PROPERTIES OF PLASTIC AND METAL

Metal can be made into sheets or thin wires. It can be melted and formed into different shapes without changing the metal itself. This makes metal a good raw material for 3-D printers. Metal also lasts a long time.

Plastics are some of the most complex materials people use. Plastics are organic materials, meaning that, like living things, they are made up of carbon and hydrogen atoms. They can occur in nature, such as the tree sap that makes natural rubber or the oil that is pumped out of the ground. People have made nonorganic plastic materials by rearranging atoms into complicated shapes called polymers.

Plastic objects are usually durable, flexible, and strong. They are easy to shape. Many do not decompose, or rot, the way wood or paper might. However, they are a source of pollution because they do not break down easily after they have been thrown away.

PRINTING BY ADDING THINGS

There are two methods by which people make objects. The first is to shape raw materials until they take on a form the person wants. This approach is called additive manufacturing. The first 3-D printers used this technique, and it is still the most common type of 3-D printing used today.

HOW IT WORKS

In additive manufacturing, the raw metal or plastic is often called a **filament**. The 3-D printer pulls this filament into a print head, which heats up the raw material until it melts. The molten material is forced through the print nozzle. It is then placed where the machine wants it to go.

Additive manufacturing works best with materials that can be melted and made solid without destroying the material. When metal or plastic are heated, they turn into liquid metal or liquid plastic and are not destroyed. After a layer of molten plastic or metal is laid down, a 3-D printer has to quickly make it solid again. If the material is thin, it cools quickly on its own. If it is thick, it can be cooled by a blast of cold air or water. The layers are built up to form an object.

CUTTING EDGE

Special types of plastic, known as **photopolymers**, turn from liquid to solid under ultraviolet light. Particular 3-D printers shine a UV laser at a container of photopolymers, turning them from a liquid to a solid. The object is then built up layer by layer.

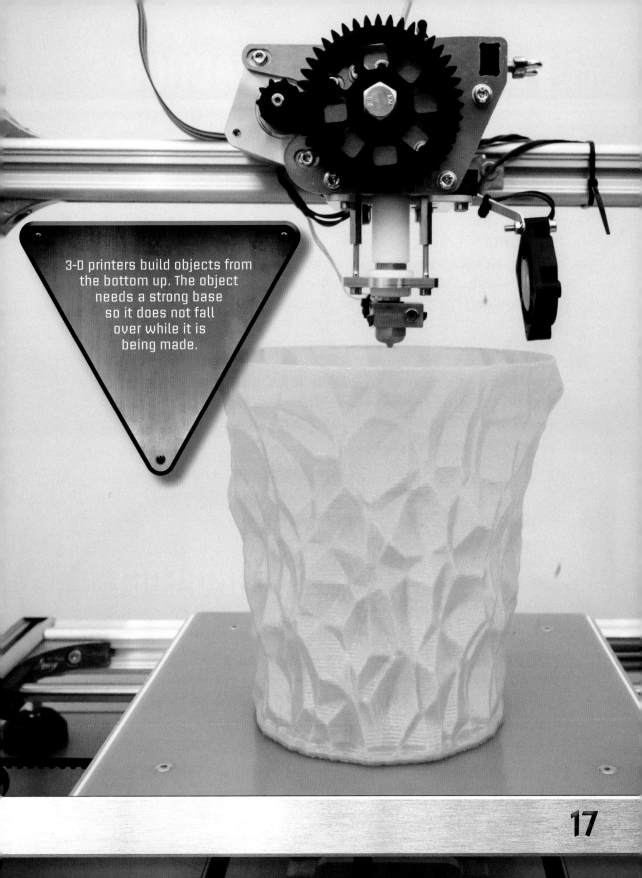

3-D printers build objects from the bottom up. The object needs a strong base so it does not fall over while it is being made.

The second method by which 3-D printers make objects is subtractive manufacturing. In subtractive manufacturing, the 3-D printer uses a block of raw material, such as wood, and carves it into a desired shape.

DRILLING

Materials such as wood, stone, and metal can be carved into delicate shapes, so they are excellent raw materials for 3-D printers. The printing device moves a high-speed drill over the surface of the material, cutting into and shaping it. A metal drill can easily cut through wood. Harder drill bits are used to cut into hard materials like stone. To cut very hard materials, such as metals, drill bits may be made of hard substances, like diamond. However, diamonds are expensive. A cheaper way to cut the metal is to spin the drill bits very quickly. This gives the drill bits the energy they need to cut into the metal material.

Subtractive manufacturing is useful because the raw material supports itself as it is carved. However, a drawback is that the size of the object made is limited by the size of the material.

CUTTING EDGE

Lasers can accurately send a huge amount of energy to a very small space. This makes them great tools for cutting and carving in subtractive manufacturing. Lasers have already been used to make precise cuts, etch, or carve, designs, and drill holes.

Stone can be chiseled into detailed carvings, but it can be difficult to control how the stone breaks under the chisel.

CHAPTER 3

COMPUTER-AIDED DESIGN

Although people have built amazing buildings from 2-D designs, it is much more difficult to program a machine to work in 3-D. Early industrial presses usually only moved up and down, for example, to press a sheet of metal into a mold. Early laser cutters also only had to move in two dimensions to drill holes or make cuts in a sheet. However, 3-D printers must move in many more directions.

AXES

A 2-D surface has length and width. The two dimensions can be shown by drawing two lines on a page. One runs from the top to the bottom, the other from the left to the right. Each line is called an axis. The line that runs from left to right is called the X-axis, while the line that runs from top to bottom is called the Y-axis. Every point on the page can be summed up as a math equation, describing where it is on the X- and Y-axis. These equations tell a laser cutter where to aim.

Working in 3-D brings in a third axis, the Z-axis. This axis meets the X- and Y-axes at a 90-degree angle and extends off the page. Instead of left and right, or top and bottom, it instructs the printer where to move forward and backward. A 3-D printer needs to know where every point of an object is on the X-axis, the Y-axis, and the Z-axis. A computer helps calculate these equations, and moves the 3-D printer accordingly.

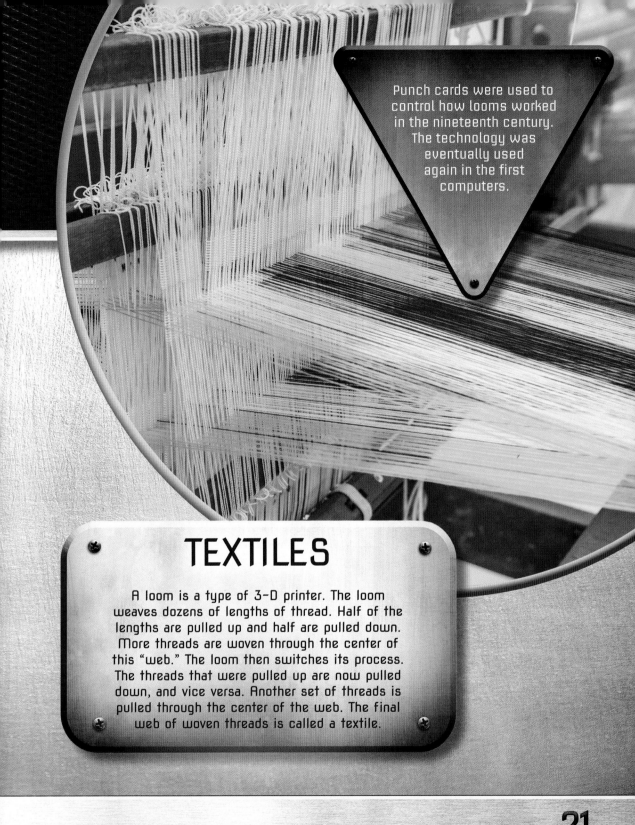

Punch cards were used to control how looms worked in the nineteenth century. The technology was eventually used again in the first computers.

TEXTILES

A loom is a type of 3-D printer. The loom weaves dozens of lengths of thread. Half of the lengths are pulled up and half are pulled down. More threads are woven through the center of this "web." The loom then switches its process. The threads that were pulled up are now pulled down, and vice versa. Another set of threads is pulled through the center of the web. The final web of woven threads is called a textile.

3-D SCANNING

Using computer-aided design, people can create virtual models of the objects they want to build on a computer. A 3-D printer can then take these models and recreate them as actual objects. To reverse the process and recreate real objects virtually on a computer requires 3-D scanning.

HOW SCANNERS WORK

3-D scanners shine laser light at an object and detect how quickly that light is reflected back. Light travels at a constant speed of 186,282 miles (299,792 km) per second. Detectors in the scanner measure the amount of time it takes between the laser light leaving its source and returning.

Another technique that 3-D scanners use is **triangulation**. Laser light is shone at a point on the object being scanned. Reflected light usually does not return directly back to the laser, so the scanner finds where the reflected light has traveled. By calculating the distance between the source of the light and its reflection and the angle at which the light traveled, a computer calculates the distance of a point.

A computer plots the locations of the points on an X, Y, and Z axis to create a computer model of the object.

CUTTING EDGE

X-rays, radio waves, or **ultrasound** waves pass through objects. Some of the energy from the ray or wave is reflected back every time it passes through a new layer of the object. This data is read by a computer and used to build a picture of what is inside an object. X-ray machines are used to look at broken bones, while MRI scanners use ultrasound waves to map the shape of the brain. Using the right software, this information can be printed by a 3-D printer.

A 3-D scanner can turn an object or has scanners that move around an object to look at it and measure it from every angle.

Digitizer
DESKTOP 3D SCANNER

One of the most useful features of 3-D printers is their versatility, or ability to adapt to many different functions. A 3-D printer can make any design that is programmed into its computer. Using the Internet and e-mail, a design created on a computer in one part of the world can be sent within seconds to a printer in a completely different part of the world. People looking for a particular design to print can find it on a website, pay for a copy, and then download it to their own printer.

UPLOAD AND DOWNLOAD

The ability to upload and download designs has created a worldwide community of people who use 3-D printers to share their inventions and ideas. For example, a website called Thingiverse is a 3-D printing site. People worldwide can upload their designs to the site or download designs from the site. They can also suggest design changes or Improvements.

CUTTING EDGE

The RepRap Project was started by Dr. Adrian Bowyer at the University of Bath, England. He imagined a 3-D printer that could print its own components, at low cost. Dr. Bowyer and his coworkers created a design that was open source, meaning that anybody can download the designs and print them. This has made 3-D printers cheaper to make and use. Hundreds of people are using the technology.

Ceramics, like this pot, are made of clay. The clay can be squeezed into place, holds its shape, and turns hard when baked.

As inventors share their discoveries with others, they inspire more exploration and new discoveries. Many inventors hope that inexpensive 3-D printing technology will help people around the world make the things they need, and thereby live better, more independent lives.

CHAPTER 4

3-D PRINTERS IN OUR LIVES

Modern 3-D printers were only invented in the early 1980s, but they are already starting to change the way we make things.

PROTOTYPES

Manufacturing companies have turned to 3-D printing to help them design and print **prototypes** of things they want to build. Before 3-D printers, car manufacturers had to make models of their products from paper or clay. Those models are now often scanned into a computer to create a virtual model. A 3-D printer can then make copies of the model. Other times, the model itself is designed on a computer, and the 3-D printer then prints it out.

VERSATILITY

3-D printing is better able to make certain objects than traditional manufacturing. Circuit boards are complex pieces of electronics that power computers. A 3-D printer can make many different types of circuit boards by laying down layers of metal in different ways, depending on the design.

The ability to print new designs as they are needed is another advantage that 3-D printers have over older machines. 3-D printers make things only when people want them, which is cheaper and less wasteful than traditional manufacturing.

Using 3-D printers, we may soon be able to print decorative objects, such as this rabbit sculpture, for our homes.

CUTTING EDGE

A Chinese company called Winsun owns one of the largest 3-D printers in the world. Its 3-D printer has a working area that is 132 feet (40 m) long, 33 feet (10 m) wide, and 22 feet (6.7 m) tall. Using recycled concrete as a raw material, the company builds furniture, houses, and even parts for five-story buildings. The company's buildings are built in one-third of the time it takes to put up a regular building.

3-D PRINTERS AND LEARNING

3-D printers can be a great help to teachers in schools. Printers are becoming cheaper, and schools can sometimes buy them for use in the classroom. Students can then learn how to program computers to print objects. They learn about measuring shapes in 3-D, and they see firsthand how structures are made.

MODELS

3-D printers can also print models for students to look at, such as 3-D maps of distant places or models of dinosaur bones. Rather than visiting a museum, a 3-D printer can bring a museum to the students. As 3-D printers become even less expensive and more versatile, people can expect to see them in more schools all around the world.

3-D printers have proven themselves to be good research tools in many areas of study. They have been used to scan and print fossils to help museums complete skeletons of dinosaurs and other ancient creatures. In cases where an artifact (an object made by a human that has historic or cultural interest) may be incomplete or lost, drawings of it can be used to create a realistic 3-D model, which shows what the artifact looked like.

3-D printed models of artifacts might be a way for visitors to not just look at them, but to also hold them in their hands or even take them home. The Metropolitan Museum in New York City and the Smithsonian Institute in Washington, D.C., offer 3-D computer models of some of their statues. People can download these designs for free and then print them using their own 3-D printers.

Computers can easily make small things several times larger. This is useful for making accurate models of things, such as the small, delicate bones of a hand.

CUTTING EDGE

Late in 2015, Washington Junior High School in Bentonville, Arkansas, was given a grant. It used the money to buy 3-D printers for its students. The students use the printers to learn about designing and programming. They have made a lot of objects, including cases for their cell phones. The school is just one of a number in Arkansas that is investing in 3-D printers to give their students experience with 3-D printing technology.

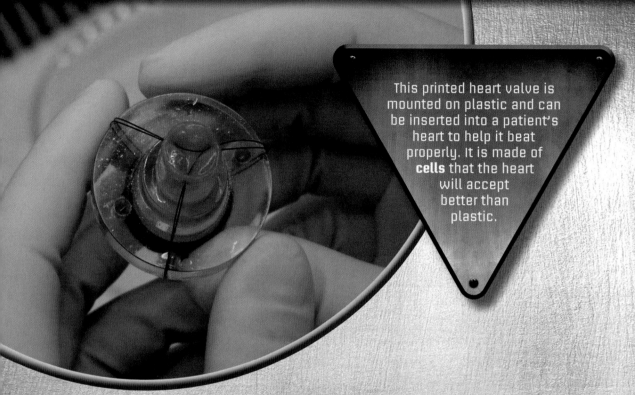

This printed heart valve is mounted on plastic and can be inserted into a patient's heart to help it beat properly. It is made of **cells** that the heart will accept better than plastic.

3-D printers have already changed the way people make artificial limbs. Prosthetic limbs used to be heavy because they were made from large blocks of wood. It was also a challenge to make the limbs fit each patient. The prosthetic limbs were so expensive that many children had to manage without them until they were adults, because they would soon outgrow any limb fitted in childhood. With 3-D printing technology, prosthetic limbs can be made so quickly and cheaply that families with children can easily get new limbs every year. The limbs they have can be redesigned or upgraded as the children grow.

TEETH, TOOLS, AND ORGANS

3-D printers have not only helped make prosthetic limbs more available, dentists use the technology to scan a patient's mouth and print dental replacements that are shaped to fit exactly. Doctors in the developing world or in isolated areas also use 3-D printers to print medical tools as they are needed. This means they do not have to buy or store expensive tools or wait for tools to be mailed to them.

3-D printing can also be used to fix problems inside the body. Scientists at Cornell University have used 3-D printers to print a new heart valve that can be shaped to an individual's heart. The device will soon be tested on sheep. Scientists at the same university have also printed cartilage, which is a type of firm-but-flexible tissue found in noses and ears. The printed cartilage could help plastic surgeons fix damaged noses and ears. Researchers at Princeton University have even printed ear cartilage with electrical parts inside that can help deaf people hear.

CUTTING EDGE

In 2015, researchers at Lawrence Livermore National Labs in California used a 3-D printer to print blood vessels that look and behave like real blood vessels. The machine uses simple cells and other biomaterials as raw materials. While these artificial blood vessels cannot yet be used in humans, they are useful for testing, and people hope that 3-D printers may soon print artificial organs for patients who need them.

3-D PRINTERS AT HOME

3-D printers are only now appearing in homes. The printers can be fun and educational, allowing parents and children to download and print models of artifacts from museums or parts for science experiments. Children can also enjoy printing toys.

Other home uses for 3-D printers include making art pieces to decorate the home, fashion accessories like bracelets and bags, or even shoes and other small items of clothing. 3-D printers are already being used to print tools for use around the home. They can also be used to print hardware, such as a missing bracket or a particular screw. Home repairs could be done a lot more quickly and easily using 3-D printing.

HOME-BUSINESSES

3-D printers can be used to launch home-businesses. A person who is good at art might create a collection to print and then sell. They could sell it at a local market and upload their designs to an online 3-D printing marketplace. 3-D printers could connect a worker to their workplace, allowing them to print small prototypes at home.

CUTTING EDGE

3-D printers can already be made into a pen that is small enough to fit into the palm of a hand. 3-D pens work in the same way as a 3-D printer, melting a plastic filament and pushing it through the tip of the pen. The user then draws in three dimensions, not only on the paper, but also in the air above it. The plastic cools and solidifies as it leaves the pen, allowing the user to doodle in three dimensions.

3-D pens can be used to draw things in three dimensions, including this model airplane.

CHAPTER 5

THE 3-D REVOLUTION

As new technologies arrive, they change the way people work, play, and interact with each other. Gutenberg's press changed the world by making books easier to produce and spreading ideas quickly. 3-D printing technology is fewer than 40 years old, but it promises to change the way we do business dramatically. Many are excited by the technology, but some people fear the changes that may result.

GOOD AND BAD

We have seen how 3-D printers make it possible for people everywhere to make goods. They no longer need to rely on stores or factories to get the things they need. Over the past decade, many people have been spending more time on the Internet, ordering goods online and shipping them to their home. While this is convenient, it does isolate people from their neighbors. Local stores sell fewer goods than online businesses, and many have gone out of business as a result. 3-D printers may only make this trend worse.

A positive of 3-D printing is that it makes it possible to run small-scale businesses anywhere. People do not have to travel to work. This saves time, which could be spent on other pursuits. 3-D printing is a developing technology. The changes that it may bring have yet to play out. We have time to make the best use of it and avoid problems before they happen.

Small town stores can suffer if people buy things online. 3-D printing may add to this—if you can make things at home, why go to the store?

CUTTING EDGE

Dutch architects are using 3-D printers to build an experimental house on a canal in Amsterdam in the Netherlands. The plan is to use recycled materials to print building blocks that can be stacked to form the walls of the house. The bricks are made of plant oil, recycled plastic, and wood fiber. The use of these materials will mean that the house generates no new waste or carbon emissions, making it better for the environment.

One place where 3-D printers could have the greatest impact is in the developing world. Many people living in countries in Africa and South America are very poor. Parts of these countries do not have roads, railroads, and power grids in the same way as wealthier nations, or the factories that they support. The technology, including medical care, that people in the developed world take for granted is not as readily available. In the past, people in the developing world have had to rely on technology imported from the developed world. By trying to improve the situation in the developing world, people have built more roads and

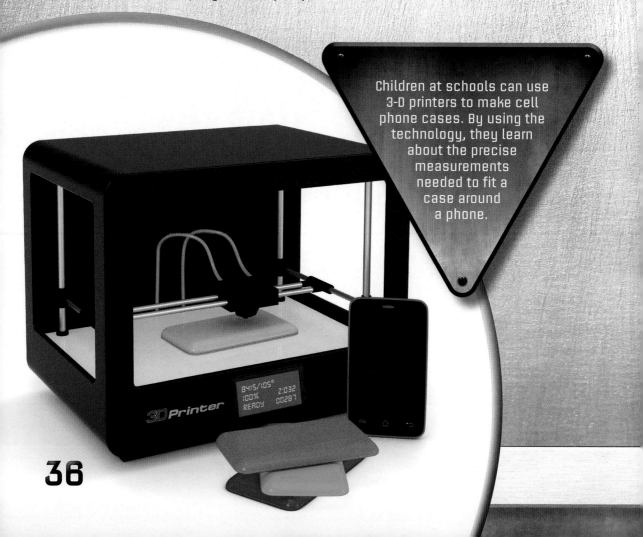

Children at schools can use 3-D printers to make cell phone cases. By using the technology, they learn about the precise measurements needed to fit a case around a phone.

factories there. Although this has led to jobs and other improvements, it has also caused problems such as pollution.

SUSTAINABILITY

3-D printers offer a cheap and **sustainable** way for people in the developing world to produce things. Communities could buy and share a number of 3-D printers. This would allow them to make the things they need locally. People could sell products from their own homes rather than having to rely on big industries. 3-D printers also use a lot less energy than large factories. The printers could be powered by small solar power units, and the raw materials could be local, recycled plastic. Best of all, 3-D printers would provide everything communities need, from tools to medical equipment.

3-D PRINTING CONCERNS

One concern about 3-D printers is how easy it is to copy things using the technology. This results in less control over what is made and by whom, and problems occur when people do not use the technology with good intentions.

Think about a toy company that sells action figures. With a 3-D printer, it is possible for a person to scan the figures and make copies of them. If the designs of the figures were then uploaded to the Internet, people could make their own figures, without ever paying the toy company that first made them.

The danger with 3-D printers is that any manufacturer, artist, or inventor could have their work copied without their permission and without payment. On the other hand, if restrictions are put in place to prevent this, artists who make sculptures of movie characters may be prevented from showing their work by the moviemakers because the sculptures could be copied using 3-D printers.

UNEMPLOYMENT?

There are also concerns that 3-D printers will replace jobs in manufacturing, putting people out of work. To deal with unemployment resulting from technological change, governments sometimes set up retraining programs to teach people how to carry out new jobs.

While it is natural to worry about the future, some concerns that people have about new technology are unfounded. 3-D printers are already a reality, but there has not been a rush of people illegally printing copyrighted goods. There have not been major job losses. However, there are well-founded concerns about the technology, and the challenge in the future will be how to manage the problems.

If other people can make things, such as sculptures, based on a person's designs using 3-D printing, how can that person make sure they are credited or paid for their work?

PRINTING GUNS

Early in 2015, a company produced plans for a 3-D printable gun before the U.S. State Department objected. This caused concern among many people who feel that the world will be a more dangerous place if people can print weapons. Other people argue that it is impossible to stop progress and people should use new technology as they wish.

CHAPTER 6

THE FUTURE

Before 1980, 3-D printers did not exist. In the early years, the printers were large and expensive. Today, many can fit on a desk, and while some large, industrial machines cost $500,000, many smaller ones can be bought for just $1,000. As the technology improves, the printers will become less expensive, and they will be found in many more homes. They will have a greater impact in our lives, and they will be able to do even more than they can do now.

Science fiction writers once imagined a type of 3-D printer called a "replicator," which could turn raw materials into complex objects, tools, and even food! 3-D printers cannot do this yet, but scientists are working toward making this a reality.

At present, 3-D printers can only print objects using one material and in one color. In the future, printers could work with more than one color and with different materials, putting them together precisely to create a perfect design.

NANOTECHNOLOGY

Some scientists think that 3-D printers may become so small that they will print tiny structures. Such printers could be injected into a body to repair cells. 3-D printers could also be programmed to make copies of themselves using the raw materials around them. These printers are called "nanobots." Some people worry that nanobots might become out of control and start making thousands of copies of themselves!

Although all new technologies raise concerns about how they could be misused, history shows that people usually adjust to new challenges and overcome them.

As the technology improves, 3-D printers will become smaller and more versatile. They will be able to create more precise and complicated designs.

CUTTING EDGE

We already use 3-D printers to make prosthetics to help people live more normal lives. Some people have asked their prosthetic makers to make very long arms that can easily reach things. Princeton University has created a 3-D printed ear inside which are electronics that help the user hear. We could use 3-D printers to create body parts that make people stronger or faster than usual. The question is, should we do this?

In the future, 3-D printers will use different raw materials. For example, spider silk, for its size, is stronger than steel, and scientists are working on ways to print spider silk. A 3-D printer already pushes out raw material in much the same way that a spider pushes out silk. 3-D printers weaving with spider silk could produce fabrics that are flexible and strong enough to stop bullets.

NANOTUBES

Carbon nanotubes, made up of special carbon atoms, are even stronger than spider silk and can **conduct** electricity better than copper. The nanotubes could be printed to make smaller, more efficient computers. 3-D printers could weave together a bunch of nanotubes into thin cables to stretch into space. They would be so strong that they could be tied to a satellite above Earth! This would create an elevator that could take people into space without the need for rockets.

Carbon nanotubes are just atoms thick. It takes 50,000 nanotubes to equal the width of one human hair.

CUTTING EDGE

3-D printing has arrived in space!
In September 2014, the International
Space Station (ISS) received a 3-D
printer that could work in the zero-gravity
environment of space. The printer is
making itself useful by printing tools for
the astronauts on board the station. If a
new wrench is needed, the 3-D printer
simply prints it. 3-D printers could one
day even print supplies astronauts
need for long-distance space
journeys, such as to Mars.

HOMES, MEDICINE, AND FOOD

With new materials, and with bigger 3-D printers, people
will be able to build bigger things. Perhaps buildings will be
printed by 3-D-printing robots, and houses, apartments, office
buildings, and even skyscrapers could be built quickly.

3-D printers could also print using organic materials, like
cells. This is called bio-printing, and it would allow doctors to
download medications. Instead of 3-D-printed plastic prosthetic
limbs, printers could instead print real limbs and even real
organs to be used in operations.

3-D printers might even be able to print food. A computer
could figure out what vitamins and nutrients a person needs,
then print food that contains them. The printers could print
a meal or an entire range of food from a supermarket.

In just 40 years, 3-D printers have changed lives. They have given people new limbs and changed the way they do business. They have helped people turn ideas into reality and build tools as they need them. The technology is still young and full of potential.

ENDLESS POSSIBILITIES

As the technology becomes cheaper and easier to use, schools, libraries, and community centers will have 3-D printers. More people will study computer-aided design and mathematics to help themselves think in 3-D. People's doodles on paper will be easily transformed into reality with 3-D printing. 3-D printers will encourage people to keep trying new ideas and to explore how things can be improved.

Artists, designers, computer makers, carpenters, and more will likely find 3-D printers become a vital part of their lives. Technology constantly evolves, and everyone can play a part. All we need is the inspiration to explore and invent. By sharing ideas and learning from others, we can help shape a future that we could once have hardly imagined.

CUTTING EDGE

Researchers at the Massachusetts Institute of Technology have created the MultiFab, a 3-D printer that works with up to 10 different materials at once. By combining many different materials, 3-D printers can print more complex objects. This is the first step toward machines that will be able to print human organs or food. We may soon be able to ask for a new cell phone, and have a 3-D printer print one for us instantly!

3-D printing helps people work together and make things at home, at school, and all around the world!

GLOSSARY

atoms the smallest particles of matter, from which molecules are made

cells the smallest functional parts of living things

conduct to take something from one place to another

filament a long, thin piece of material, like a thread

lamination a process in which layers are built up with glue into a desired shape

molecules particles made up of more than one atom

photopolymers plastic materials that react to bright light and change state from liquid to solid

polymers materials made from a large number of complicated molecules, usually found in plastic and rubber

prosthetic an artificial body part

prototypes early models of a design, from which other designs are developed

sintering a process in which something is made by compressing and melting a fine powder into a solid object

smelting a process that takes a metal ore and heats the rock until the metal melts and separates from the rock

sustainable the ability to use resources in such a way that prevents the resources from running out in the future

triangulation using a series of triangles to determine where something is

ultrasound sound waves that are so high pitched they are beyond the range of human hearing

ultraviolet light that has more energy than visible light

FOR MORE INFORMATION

BOOKS

Diana, Carla. *LEO the Maker Prince: Journeys in 3D Printing.* Sebastopol, CA: Maker Media, 2013.

Murphy, Maggie. *High-Tech DIY Projects with 3D Printing* (Maker Kids). New York, NY: PowerKids Press, 2014.

O'Neill, Terence, and Josh Williams. *3D Printing* (21st Century Skills Innovation Library: Makers as Innovators). North Mankato, MN: Cherry Lake, 2013.

Petrikowski, Nicki Peter. *Getting the Most Out of Makerspaces to Create with 3-D Printers.* New York, NY: Rosen Group, 2014.

WEBSITES

Find links to apps, tools, and tutorials to get involved in the world of 3-D printing at:
kidscreationstation.com/resources/3d-printing-resources-4-kids

Watch videos, design projects, and play games to find out more about 3-D printing at:
pbskids.org/designsquad

Try out 3-D modeling ideas at:
www.tinkercad.com

INDEX